T5-CQC-300

What's the use? Yesterday an egg,
tomorrow a feather duster.

—MARK FENDERSON

Can anybody remember when the times were not hard and money not scarce?

—RALPH W. EMERSON

Up! up! my friend, and clear your
        looks;
Why all this toil and trouble?

—WILLIAM WORDSWORTH

'Tis always morning somewhere in the world.

—RICHARD HORNE

I'VE HAD TROUBLES, TOO...

SO I BROUGHT YOU THIS BOOK

I'VE HAD TROUBLES, TOO...

SO I BROUGHT YOU THIS BOOK

Compiled by
KEITH FALLON

STANYAN BOOKS   RANDOM HOUSE

Copyright ©, 1972, by
Montcalm Productions, Inc.

All rights reserved under
International Copyright Laws.

A Stanyan Book
Published by Stanyan Books,
8721 Sunset Blvd., Suite C
Hollywood, California 90069
and by Random House, Inc.
201 East 50th Street,
New York, N.Y. 10022

Library of Congress Catalog
Card Number: 72-81617

ISBN: 0-394-48218-2

Printed in U.S.A.

Designed by Hy Fujita

Life ain't all beer and skittles.

—GEORGE DU MAURIER

Life is a predicament which
precedes death.

—HENRY JAMES

The first hundred years are the
hardest.

—WILSON MIZNER

The world is like a board with
holes in it, and the square men
have got into the round holes, and
the round into the square.

—GEORGE BERKELEY

There is only the difference of a letter between the beginning and the end — creation and cremation.

—SIR HERBERT BEERBOHM TREE

Life's a tumble-about thing of ups and downs.

—BENJAMIN DISRAELI

No matter how thin you slice it, it's still baloney.

—ALFRED E. SMITH

There's a certain melancholy in watching yourself rot.

—KATHARINE HEPBURN

Now I am beginning to live a little,
and feel less like a sick oyster at
low tide.

—LOUISA M. ALCOTT

The whole of my life has passed
like a razor—in hot water or a
scrape.

—SYDNEY SMITH

COUNT YOUR BLESSINGS —
(Unless you're a hippie)

A medical journal reports that today's hippies are afflicted with yesterday's ills. These include nagging navels caused by large belt buckles, itching heads and "vagabond skin," both the latter because of a dearth of bathing. Headbands produce a rash that's been rare since we ceased wearing hats.

There is also a <u>new</u> problem: those allergic to marijuana develop a condition called flannel mouth.

God makes all things good; man meddles with them and they become evil.

—JEAN JACQUES ROUSSEAU

Everybody thinks there's some secret out there in the world, but I've looked and I know there isn't. As long as you go on thinking it's there, the longer you miss the nice things in life—the smell of a bakery, the laughter of friends, things like that.

—BARRY NELSON

Nearly all men die of their remedies, and not of their illnesses.

—MOLIERE

Life is a stream upon which drift flowers in spring, and blocks of ice in winter.

—JOSEPH ROUX

Ask yourself whether you are happy, and you cease to be so.

—JOHN STUART MILL

Man is a rope stretched between
the animal and the Superman — a
rope over an abyss.

—FRIEDRICH NIETZSCHE

The great business of life is to be, to do, to do without, and to depart.

—JOHN MORLEY

A man must take the fat with the lean; that's what he must make up his mind to in this life.

—CHARLES DICKENS

If the grass is greener in the other fellow's yard, let him worry about cutting it.

—FRED ALLEN

Never play cards with a man called Doc. Never eat at a place called Mom's.

—NELSON ALGREN

One who longs for death is
miserable, but more miserable is
he who fears it.

—JULIUS ZINCGREF

Worry, the interest paid by those
who borrow trouble.

—GEORGE W. LYON

Some people are so fond of ill
luck that they run halfway to meet
it.

—DOUGLAS JERROLD

Man is not the creature of
circumstances. Circumstances
are the creatures of men.

—BENJAMIN DISRAELI

It is a pity that we cannot escape
from life when we are young.

—MARK TWAIN

Except during the nine months
before he draws his first breath,
no man manages his affairs as
well as a tree does.

—BERNARD SHAW

My mother was accursed the
    night she bore me,
and I am faint with envy of all
    the dead.

—EURIPIDES
Alcestis

I never married, and I wish my
father never had.

—BEVINS JAY

I wish either my father or my
mother, or indeed both of them…
had minded what they were about
when they begot me.

—LAURENCE STERNE

Life is a jest, and all things
        show it:
I thought so once, but now I
        know it.

—JOHN GAY
  My Own Epitaph

She tried—
But she died.

—JANE WILKIE
  Her own epitaph

I advise you to go on living solely
to enrage those who are paying
your annuities. It is the only
pleasure I have left.

—VOLTAIRE

Never trouble trouble till trouble
troubles you.

—NELLIE MELBA (among others)

All human wisdom is summed up
in two words—wait and hope.

—ALEXANDRE DUMAS THE ELDER

When the Great Scorer comes to
    write against your name —
He marks — not that you won or
    lost — but how you played
    the game.

                    —GRANTLAND RICE

I think about the distance to doubt
and find it's too far to go.

                    —ROD McKUEN

Never answer a telephone that
rings before breakfast.

                    —JAMES THURBER

SOME PEOPLE MAKE IT...

During the month of November in 1971:

ELIZABETH II

Having asked Parliament to double her annual salary of $2.45 million, Queen Elizabeth wasted no time in waiting for a decision. She went into the apple business, selling fruit to the public at Sandringham, her estate in Norfolk.

ELIZABETH, TOO

Feeling no pinch from the recession, Elizabeth Taylor appeared at a ball outside Paris, wearing $3 million worth of jewels. A 20-carat emerald supported a headdress of plumes, the headband on her forehead sported 1000 small diamonds along with 25 big ones. At her throat was the $1 million diamond given her by Richard Burton.

ON THE OTHER HAND

A judge ruled in favor of Francis J. Colleta, who complained a parking meter had robbed him of 20 cents. But to get a copy of the judgment, Colleta had to pay the court 50 cents.

Double, double toil and trouble;
Fire burn and cauldron bubble.

—WILLIAM SHAKESPEARE
Macbeth

The thought of suicide is a great consolation: by means of it one gets successfully through many a bad night.

—FRIEDRICH NIETZSCHE

…see that ye be not troubled: for all these things must come to pass…

—MATTHEW 24:6

I have had troubles in my life but the worst of them never came.

—JAMES A. GARFIELD

Things are in the saddle, and
ride mankind.

—RALPH W. EMERSON

Nice guys finish last.

—LEO DUROCHER

Misfortunes and twins never come singly.

—JOSH BILLINGS

A peck of troubles.

—DESIDERIUS ERASMUS

A little sunburnt by the glare of life.

—ELIZABETH BARRETT BROWNING

Big fleas have little fleas
    to plague, perplex and bite 'em.
Little fleas have lesser fleas,
    and so <u>ad</u> <u>infinitum</u>.

—R. R. FIELDER

Whether 'tis nobler in the mind
    to suffer
The slings and arrows of
    outrageous fortune,
Or to take arms against a sea
    of troubles,
And by opposing, end them?

—WILLIAM SHAKESPEARE
Hamlet

We are all Charlie Brown.

—ALEXANDER DREY

If life had a second edition, how I would correct the proofs!

—JOHN CLARE

Everyone has his day, and some days last longer than others.

—WINSTON CHURCHILL

In all ages the wisest have always
agreed in their judgment of life:
<u>it</u> <u>is</u> <u>no</u> <u>good</u>.

—FRIEDRICH NIETZSCHE

Life is like a scrambled egg.

—DON MARQUIS

Youth is a blunder; manhood a
struggle; old age a regret.

—BENJAMIN DISRAELI

Life is a one way street.

—BERNARD BERENSON

Pigeons on the grass alas.

—GERTRUDE STEIN

Goodbye, proud world! I'm
   going home;
Thou are not my friend
   and I'm not thine.

—RALPH W. EMERSON

Life is made up of marble and mud.

—NATHANIEL HAWTHORNE

Indigestion is charged by God with enforcing morality on the stomach.

—VICTOR HUGO

Our days begin with trouble here,
Our life is but a span,
And cruel death is always near,
So frail a thing is man.

— The New England Primer

But somewhere, beyond Space
    and Time,
Is wetter water, slimier slime!

—RUPERT BROOKE
Heaven

You buy some flowers for your
      table;
You tend them tenderly as you're
      able;
You fetch them water from
      hither and thither —
What thanks do you get for it all?
      They wither.

                    — SAMUEL HOFFENSTEIN

Man is born into trouble, as the
sparks fly upward.

—JOB 5:7

A romantic is one who, when life is
too banal or too lazy to
manufacture tragedy for him,
creates it artificially, thus getting
himself into the hot water he
himself has boiled.

—CLIFTON FADIMAN

I am troubled, I'm dissatisfied,
I'm Irish.

—MARIANNE MOORE
Spenser's Ireland

I don't mind being burdened with
being glamorous and sexual.

—MARILYN MONROE

Life is like a B-picture script. It's
that corny. If I had my life story
offered to me to film, I'd turn it
down.

—KIRK DOUGLAS

Borrow trouble for yourself, if that's your nature, but don't lend it to your neighbors.

—RUDYARD KIPLING

The reason worry kills more people than work is that more people worry than work.

—ROBERT FROST

Never go out to meet trouble. If you will just sit still, nine times out of ten someone will intercept it before it reaches you.

—CALVIN COOLIDGE

Life is one damned thing after another.

—FRANK O'MALLEY

For most men, life is a search for the proper manila envelope in which to get themselves filed.

—CLIFTON FADIMAN

Life is made up of sobs, sniffles and smiles, with sniffles predominating.

— O. HENRY

Worry makes everybody thin except fat people who worry over their fatness.

— Reflections of a Bachelor

You may be as vicious about me as you please. You will only do me justice.

— RICHARD BURTON

A hole is nothing at all, but you can break your neck in it.

— AUSTIN O'MALLEY

In trouble to be troubled
Is to have your trouble doubled.

-DANIEL DEFOE

Most of our misfortunes are more supportable than the comments of our friends upon them.

-CALEB COLTON

You went to some trouble to be born, and that's all.

-PIERRE DE BEAUMARCHAIS

Life can only be understood
backwards; but it must be lived
forwards.

—SÖREN KIERKEGAARD

Better a louse in the pot than no
flesh at all.

—JOHN CLARKE

Nothing in life is so exhilarating as
to be shot at without result.

—WINSTON CHURCHILL

The strangest whim has seized
      me
      …After all
I think I will not hang myself today.

—G. K. CHESTERTON
A Ballad of Suicide

The only limit to our realization of tomorrow will be our doubts of today. Let us move forward with strong and active faith.

—FRANKLIN D. ROOSEVELT

Life is short; live it up.

—NIKITA KHRUSHCHEV